Welcome to your new garden diary. We put a lot of thought into it; we hope you get as much pleasure using it as we did creating it.

The first few pages assist you in clarifying plans for the year ahead. You'll find space to jot down ideas, make final decisions, sketch designs on graphing paper and block out the year's work on an at-a-glance calendar.

The majority of the book is the weekly diary. It's purposely big, so that each week fits to a page and allows for both forward planning and retrospective journaling without being tight on space. We give no apology for making this a 'start-any-time' diary. Our first thought was to have the book run from January to January, but the inspiration to begin a garden diary can hit at any time. No one wants to buy diary space that has already passed and will never be used, so a 'start-any-time' layout was the obvious solution. The trade-off, of course, is that the owner has to fill in the name of each month, but we've prevented filling-in from becoming at all laborious by numbering each week for you; (there's always a week 5 just in case you need it.) You can record the week start date should you wish, but it's not a necessity, just skip it (or any other record box) if you want to – always be the master of your garden diary and not the other way round! Don't let it constrain you. For instance, in your monthly round-up, do journal visits to other gardens as well as lessons learned in yours. The diary is very much intended to be a keepsake with plenty of space for pictures and memories of time spent in the garden with family and friends.

Finally, at the back you'll find a few Appendices to store plant lists, supplier details, and, last but not least, a 'brainstorming' space for future years.

We do hope you enjoy your garden this year,

Best wishes,

The smART bookx design team

Plans for the Year

Final Decisions

This is a brainstorming page. Use the grey border boxes to bring together any ideas or inspirations you currently have for your garden, no matter how unsure you are about them. Then, collect your thoughts and make your final decisions for the coming year. Use Appendix III, which is similar to this page, to store ideas for future years.

At-a-glance Year Planner

	Job 1:	Job 2:	Job 3:	Job 4:	Job 5:
January					
February					
March					
April					
May					
June					
July					
August					
September					
October					
November					
December					
January					
February					
March					
April					
May					
June					
July					
August					
September					
October					
November					
December					

Continued ...

	Job 6:	Job 7:	Job 8:	Job 9:	Job 10:
January					
February					
March					
April					
May					
June					
July					
August					
September					
October					
November					
December					
January					
February					
March					
April					
May					
June					
July					
August					
September					
October					
November					
December					

Use this space to affix photographs or make sketches of your garden as is looks now.

MONTH

Jobs this Month

○ _____
_____
○ _____
_____
○ _____
_____
○ _____
_____
○ _____
_____
○ _____
_____
○ _____
_____
○ _____
_____
○ _____
_____
○ _____
_____
○ _____
_____

MONTH

MONTH

Week 1

Start Date

Weather

Wildlife

Blooms

Highlight

Things to Do

Planting
☆ ○
☆ ○
☆ ○
☆ ○
☆ ○
☆ ○

Propagation
☆ ○
☆ ○
☆ ○
☆ ○
☆ ○
☆ ○

Pruning
☆ ○
☆ ○
☆ ○
☆ ○
☆ ○
☆ ○

Maintenance
☆ ○
☆ ○
☆ ○
☆ ○
☆ ○
☆ ○

Pest Control
☆ ○
☆ ○
☆ ○
☆ ○
☆ ○
☆ ○

Other
☆ ○
☆ ○
☆ ○
☆ ○
☆ ○
☆ ○

Purchasing	Cost

Harvesting	Amount

Weekly Journal

Things to Do

Planting
☆ _____ ○
☆ _____ ○
☆ _____ ○
☆ _____ ○
☆ _____ ○
☆ _____ ○

Propagation
☆ _____ ○
☆ _____ ○
☆ _____ ○
☆ _____ ○
☆ _____ ○
☆ _____ ○

Pruning
☆ _____ ○
☆ _____ ○
☆ _____ ○
☆ _____ ○
☆ _____ ○
☆ _____ ○

Maintenance
☆ _____ ○
☆ _____ ○
☆ _____ ○
☆ _____ ○
☆ _____ ○
☆ _____ ○

Pest Control
☆ _____ ○
☆ _____ ○
☆ _____ ○
☆ _____ ○
☆ _____ ○
☆ _____ ○

Other
☆ _____ ○
☆ _____ ○
☆ _____ ○
☆ _____ ○
☆ _____ ○
☆ _____ ○

Purchasing	Cost
_____	
_____	
_____	
_____	
_____	

Harvesting	Amount
_____	
_____	
_____	
_____	
_____	

Weekly Journal

MONTH

Week 2

Start Date

Weather

Wildlife

Blooms

Highlight

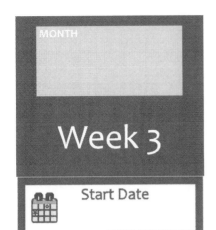

MONTH

Week 3

Start Date

Weather

Wildlife

Blooms

Highlight

Things to Do

Planting
☆ _____ ○
☆ _____ ○
☆ _____ ○
☆ _____ ○
☆ _____ ○
☆ _____ ○

Propagation
☆ _____ ○
☆ _____ ○
☆ _____ ○
☆ _____ ○
☆ _____ ○
☆ _____ ○

Pruning
☆ _____ ○
☆ _____ ○
☆ _____ ○
☆ _____ ○
☆ _____ ○
☆ _____ ○

Maintenance
☆ _____ ○
☆ _____ ○
☆ _____ ○
☆ _____ ○
☆ _____ ○
☆ _____ ○

Pest Control
☆ _____ ○
☆ _____ ○
☆ _____ ○
☆ _____ ○
☆ _____ ○
☆ _____ ○

Other
☆ _____ ○
☆ _____ ○
☆ _____ ○
☆ _____ ○
☆ _____ ○
☆ _____ ○

Purchasing	Cost

Harvesting	Amount

Weekly Journal

Things to Do

Planting
☆ _____ ○
☆ _____ ○
☆ _____ ○
☆ _____ ○
☆ _____ ○
☆ _____ ○

Propagation
☆ _____ ○
☆ _____ ○
☆ _____ ○
☆ _____ ○
☆ _____ ○
☆ _____ ○

Pruning
☆ _____ ○
☆ _____ ○
☆ _____ ○
☆ _____ ○
☆ _____ ○
☆ _____ ○

Maintenance
☆ _____ ○
☆ _____ ○
☆ _____ ○
☆ _____ ○
☆ _____ ○
☆ _____ ○

Pest Control
☆ _____ ○
☆ _____ ○
☆ _____ ○
☆ _____ ○
☆ _____ ○
☆ _____ ○

Other
☆ _____ ○
☆ _____ ○
☆ _____ ○
☆ _____ ○
☆ _____ ○
☆ _____ ○

Purchasing   Cost

Harvesting   Amount

Weekly Journal

MONTH

Week 4

Start Date

Weather

Wildlife

Blooms

Highlight

MONTH

Week 5

Start Date

Weather

Wildlife

Blooms

Highlight

Things to Do

Planting
☆ .... ○
☆ .... ○
☆ .... ○
☆ .... ○
☆ .... ○
☆ .... ○

Propagation
☆ .... ○
☆ .... ○
☆ .... ○
☆ .... ○
☆ .... ○
☆ .... ○

Pruning
☆ .... ○
☆ .... ○
☆ .... ○
☆ .... ○
☆ .... ○
☆ .... ○

Maintenance
☆ .... ○
☆ .... ○
☆ .... ○
☆ .... ○
☆ .... ○
☆ .... ○

Pest Control
☆ .... ○
☆ .... ○
☆ .... ○
☆ .... ○
☆ .... ○
☆ .... ○

Other
☆ .... ○
☆ .... ○
☆ .... ○
☆ .... ○
☆ .... ○
☆ .... ○

Purchasing	Cost

Harvesting	Amount

Weekly Journal

Monthly Roundup

Use this space to affix photographs or make sketches of your garden as is looks now.

Jobs this Month

○ ....
....
○ ....
....
○ ....
....
○ ....
....
○ ....
....
○ ....
....
○ ....
....
○ ....
....
○ ....
....
○ ....
....
○ ....
....

MONTH

Week 1

Start Date

Weather

Wildlife

Blooms

Highlight

Things to Do

Planting
- ☆ _____ ○
- ☆ _____ ○
- ☆ _____ ○
- ☆ _____ ○
- ☆ _____ ○
- ☆ _____ ○

Propagation
- ☆ _____ ○
- ☆ _____ ○
- ☆ _____ ○
- ☆ _____ ○
- ☆ _____ ○
- ☆ _____ ○

Pruning
- ☆ _____ ○
- ☆ _____ ○
- ☆ _____ ○
- ☆ _____ ○
- ☆ _____ ○
- ☆ _____ ○

Maintenance
- ☆ _____ ○
- ☆ _____ ○
- ☆ _____ ○
- ☆ _____ ○
- ☆ _____ ○
- ☆ _____ ○

Pest Control
- ☆ _____ ○
- ☆ _____ ○
- ☆ _____ ○
- ☆ _____ ○
- ☆ _____ ○
- ☆ _____ ○

Other
- ☆ _____ ○
- ☆ _____ ○
- ☆ _____ ○
- ☆ _____ ○
- ☆ _____ ○
- ☆ _____ ○

Purchasing	Cost

Harvesting	Amount

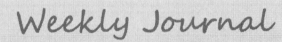

Weekly Journal

Things to Do

Planting
☆ _____ ○
☆ _____ ○
☆ _____ ○
☆ _____ ○
☆ _____ ○
☆ _____ ○

Propagation
☆ _____ ○
☆ _____ ○
☆ _____ ○
☆ _____ ○
☆ _____ ○
☆ _____ ○

Pruning
☆ _____ ○
☆ _____ ○
☆ _____ ○
☆ _____ ○
☆ _____ ○
☆ _____ ○

Maintenance
☆ _____ ○
☆ _____ ○
☆ _____ ○
☆ _____ ○
☆ _____ ○
☆ _____ ○

Pest Control
☆ _____ ○
☆ _____ ○
☆ _____ ○
☆ _____ ○
☆ _____ ○
☆ _____ ○

Other
☆ _____ ○
☆ _____ ○
☆ _____ ○
☆ _____ ○
☆ _____ ○
☆ _____ ○

Purchasing   Cost
_____
_____
_____
_____
_____

Harvesting   Amount
_____
_____
_____
_____
_____

Weekly Journal

MONTH

Week 2

Start Date

Weather

Wildlife

Blooms

Highlight

MONTH

Week 3

Start Date

Weather

Wildlife

Blooms

Highlight

Things to Do

Planting	Propagation	Pruning
☆ _____ ○	☆ _____ ○	☆ _____ ○
☆ _____ ○	☆ _____ ○	☆ _____ ○
☆ _____ ○	☆ _____ ○	☆ _____ ○
☆ _____ ○	☆ _____ ○	☆ _____ ○
☆ _____ ○	☆ _____ ○	☆ _____ ○
☆ _____ ○	☆ _____ ○	☆ _____ ○

Maintenance	Pest Control	Other
☆ _____ ○	☆ _____ ○	☆ _____ ○
☆ _____ ○	☆ _____ ○	☆ _____ ○
☆ _____ ○	☆ _____ ○	☆ _____ ○
☆ _____ ○	☆ _____ ○	☆ _____ ○
☆ _____ ○	☆ _____ ○	☆ _____ ○
☆ _____ ○	☆ _____ ○	☆ _____ ○

Purchasing	Cost

Harvesting	Amount

Weekly Journal

Things to Do

Planting
☆ .... ○
☆ .... ○
☆ .... ○
☆ .... ○
☆ .... ○
☆ .... ○

Propagation
☆ .... ○
☆ .... ○
☆ .... ○
☆ .... ○
☆ .... ○
☆ .... ○

Pruning
☆ .... ○
☆ .... ○
☆ .... ○
☆ .... ○
☆ .... ○
☆ .... ○

Maintenance
☆ .... ○
☆ .... ○
☆ .... ○
☆ .... ○
☆ .... ○
☆ .... ○

Pest Control
☆ .... ○
☆ .... ○
☆ .... ○
☆ .... ○
☆ .... ○
☆ .... ○

Other
☆ .... ○
☆ .... ○
☆ .... ○
☆ .... ○
☆ .... ○
☆ .... ○

Purchasing — Cost

Harvesting — Amount

Weekly Journal

MONTH

Week 4

📅 Start Date

Weather

Wildlife

Blooms

Highlight

Week 5

MONTH

Start Date

Weather

Wildlife

Blooms

Highlight

Things to Do

Planting
☆ _____ ○
☆ _____ ○
☆ _____ ○
☆ _____ ○
☆ _____ ○
☆ _____ ○

Propagation
☆ _____ ○
☆ _____ ○
☆ _____ ○
☆ _____ ○
☆ _____ ○
☆ _____ ○

Pruning
☆ _____ ○
☆ _____ ○
☆ _____ ○
☆ _____ ○
☆ _____ ○
☆ _____ ○

Maintenance
☆ _____ ○
☆ _____ ○
☆ _____ ○
☆ _____ ○
☆ _____ ○
☆ _____ ○

Pest Control
☆ _____ ○
☆ _____ ○
☆ _____ ○
☆ _____ ○
☆ _____ ○
☆ _____ ○

Other
☆ _____ ○
☆ _____ ○
☆ _____ ○
☆ _____ ○
☆ _____ ○
☆ _____ ○

Purchasing	Cost

Harvesting	Amount

Weekly Journal

Monthly Roundup

Use this space to affix photographs or make sketches of your garden as is looks now.

Jobs this Month

○ ....

○ ....

○ ....

○ ....

○ ....

○ ....

○ ....

○ ....

○ ....

○ ....

○ ....

○ ....

○ ....

MONTH

Week 1

Start Date

Weather

Wildlife

Blooms

Highlight

Things to Do

Planting
☆ ○
☆ ○
☆ ○
☆ ○
☆ ○
☆ ○

Propagation
☆ ○
☆ ○
☆ ○
☆ ○
☆ ○
☆ ○

Pruning
☆ ○
☆ ○
☆ ○
☆ ○
☆ ○
☆ ○

Maintenance
☆ ○
☆ ○
☆ ○
☆ ○
☆ ○
☆ ○

Pest Control
☆ ○
☆ ○
☆ ○
☆ ○
☆ ○
☆ ○

Other
☆ ○
☆ ○
☆ ○
☆ ○
☆ ○
☆ ○

Purchasing	Cost

Harvesting	Amount

Weekly Journal

Things to Do

Planting
- ☆ .... ○
- ☆ .... ○
- ☆ .... ○
- ☆ .... ○
- ☆ .... ○
- ☆ .... ○

Propagation
- ☆ .... ○
- ☆ .... ○
- ☆ .... ○
- ☆ .... ○
- ☆ .... ○
- ☆ .... ○

Pruning
- ☆ .... ○
- ☆ .... ○
- ☆ .... ○
- ☆ .... ○
- ☆ .... ○
- ☆ .... ○

Maintenance
- ☆ .... ○
- ☆ .... ○
- ☆ .... ○
- ☆ .... ○
- ☆ .... ○
- ☆ .... ○

Pest Control
- ☆ .... ○
- ☆ .... ○
- ☆ .... ○
- ☆ .... ○
- ☆ .... ○
- ☆ .... ○

Other
- ☆ .... ○
- ☆ .... ○
- ☆ .... ○
- ☆ .... ○
- ☆ .... ○
- ☆ .... ○

Start Date

Weather

Purchasing	Cost

Harvesting	Amount

Wildlife

Blooms

Weekly Journal

Highlight

MONTH

Week 3

Start Date

Weather

Wildlife

Blooms

Highlight

Things to Do

Planting
☆ _____ ○
☆ _____ ○
☆ _____ ○
☆ _____ ○
☆ _____ ○
☆ _____ ○

Propagation
☆ _____ ○
☆ _____ ○
☆ _____ ○
☆ _____ ○
☆ _____ ○
☆ _____ ○

Pruning
☆ _____ ○
☆ _____ ○
☆ _____ ○
☆ _____ ○
☆ _____ ○
☆ _____ ○

Maintenance
☆ _____ ○
☆ _____ ○
☆ _____ ○
☆ _____ ○
☆ _____ ○
☆ _____ ○

Pest Control
☆ _____ ○
☆ _____ ○
☆ _____ ○
☆ _____ ○
☆ _____ ○
☆ _____ ○

Other
☆ _____ ○
☆ _____ ○
☆ _____ ○
☆ _____ ○
☆ _____ ○
☆ _____ ○

Purchasing	Cost

Harvesting	Amount

Weekly Journal

Things to Do

Planting
☆ .... ○
☆ .... ○
☆ .... ○
☆ .... ○
☆ .... ○
☆ .... ○

Propagation
☆ .... ○
☆ .... ○
☆ .... ○
☆ .... ○
☆ .... ○
☆ .... ○

Pruning
☆ .... ○
☆ .... ○
☆ .... ○
☆ .... ○
☆ .... ○
☆ .... ○

Maintenance
☆ .... ○
☆ .... ○
☆ .... ○
☆ .... ○
☆ .... ○
☆ .... ○

Pest Control
☆ .... ○
☆ .... ○
☆ .... ○
☆ .... ○
☆ .... ○
☆ .... ○

Other
☆ .... ○
☆ .... ○
☆ .... ○
☆ .... ○
☆ .... ○
☆ .... ○

Purchasing | Cost

Harvesting | Amount

Weekly Journal

MONTH

Week 4

Start Date

Weather

Wildlife

Blooms

Highlight

MONTH

Week 5

Start Date

Weather

Wildlife

Blooms

Highlight

Things to Do

Planting
☆ _____ ○
☆ _____ ○
☆ _____ ○
☆ _____ ○
☆ _____ ○
☆ _____ ○

Propagation
☆ _____ ○
☆ _____ ○
☆ _____ ○
☆ _____ ○
☆ _____ ○
☆ _____ ○

Pruning
☆ _____ ○
☆ _____ ○
☆ _____ ○
☆ _____ ○
☆ _____ ○
☆ _____ ○

Maintenance
☆ _____ ○
☆ _____ ○
☆ _____ ○
☆ _____ ○
☆ _____ ○
☆ _____ ○

Pest Control
☆ _____ ○
☆ _____ ○
☆ _____ ○
☆ _____ ○
☆ _____ ○
☆ _____ ○

Other
☆ _____ ○
☆ _____ ○
☆ _____ ○
☆ _____ ○
☆ _____ ○
☆ _____ ○

Purchasing	Cost

Harvesting	Amount

Weekly Journal

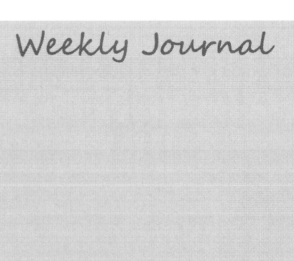

Monthly Roundup

Use this space to affix photographs or make sketches of your garden as is looks now.

Jobs this Month

○ ....
○ ....
○ ....
○ ....
○ ....
○ ....
○ ....
○ ....
○ ....
○ ....
○ ....

MONTH

Week 1

Start Date

Weather

Wildlife

Blooms

Highlight

Things to Do

Planting
☆ ○
☆ ○
☆ ○
☆ ○
☆ ○
☆ ○

Propagation
☆ ○
☆ ○
☆ ○
☆ ○
☆ ○
☆ ○

Pruning
☆ ○
☆ ○
☆ ○
☆ ○
☆ ○
☆ ○

Maintenance
☆ ○
☆ ○
☆ ○
☆ ○
☆ ○
☆ ○

Pest Control
☆ ○
☆ ○
☆ ○
☆ ○
☆ ○
☆ ○

Other
☆ ○
☆ ○
☆ ○
☆ ○
☆ ○
☆ ○

Purchasing	Cost

Harvesting	Amount

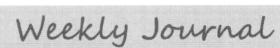

Weekly Journal

Things to Do

Planting
☆ _____ ○
☆ _____ ○
☆ _____ ○
☆ _____ ○
☆ _____ ○
☆ _____ ○

Propagation
☆ _____ ○
☆ _____ ○
☆ _____ ○
☆ _____ ○
☆ _____ ○
☆ _____ ○

Pruning
☆ _____ ○
☆ _____ ○
☆ _____ ○
☆ _____ ○
☆ _____ ○
☆ _____ ○

Maintenance
☆ _____ ○
☆ _____ ○
☆ _____ ○
☆ _____ ○
☆ _____ ○
☆ _____ ○

Pest Control
☆ _____ ○
☆ _____ ○
☆ _____ ○
☆ _____ ○
☆ _____ ○
☆ _____ ○

Other
☆ _____ ○
☆ _____ ○
☆ _____ ○
☆ _____ ○
☆ _____ ○
☆ _____ ○

Purchasing	Cost
....	
....	
....	
....	
....	

Harvesting	Amount
....	
....	
....	
....	
....	

Weekly Journal

MONTH

Week 2

Start Date

Weather

Wildlife

Blooms

Highlight

MONTH

Week 3

Start Date

Weather

Wildlife

Blooms

Highlight

MONTH

Things to Do

Planting
☆ _____ ○
☆ _____ ○
☆ _____ ○
☆ _____ ○
☆ _____ ○
☆ _____ ○

Propagation
☆ _____ ○
☆ _____ ○
☆ _____ ○
☆ _____ ○
☆ _____ ○
☆ _____ ○

Pruning
☆ _____ ○
☆ _____ ○
☆ _____ ○
☆ _____ ○
☆ _____ ○
☆ _____ ○

Maintenance
☆ _____ ○
☆ _____ ○
☆ _____ ○
☆ _____ ○
☆ _____ ○
☆ _____ ○

Pest Control
☆ _____ ○
☆ _____ ○
☆ _____ ○
☆ _____ ○
☆ _____ ○
☆ _____ ○

Other
☆ _____ ○
☆ _____ ○
☆ _____ ○
☆ _____ ○
☆ _____ ○
☆ _____ ○

Purchasing — Cost

Harvesting — Amount

Weekly Journal

Things to Do

Planting
☆ ⋯⋯⋯⋯⋯⋯⋯⋯ ○
☆ ⋯⋯⋯⋯⋯⋯⋯⋯ ○
☆ ⋯⋯⋯⋯⋯⋯⋯⋯ ○
☆ ⋯⋯⋯⋯⋯⋯⋯⋯ ○
☆ ⋯⋯⋯⋯⋯⋯⋯⋯ ○
☆ ⋯⋯⋯⋯⋯⋯⋯⋯ ○

Propagation
☆ ⋯⋯⋯⋯⋯⋯⋯⋯ ○
☆ ⋯⋯⋯⋯⋯⋯⋯⋯ ○
☆ ⋯⋯⋯⋯⋯⋯⋯⋯ ○
☆ ⋯⋯⋯⋯⋯⋯⋯⋯ ○
☆ ⋯⋯⋯⋯⋯⋯⋯⋯ ○
☆ ⋯⋯⋯⋯⋯⋯⋯⋯ ○

Pruning
☆ ⋯⋯⋯⋯⋯⋯⋯⋯ ○
☆ ⋯⋯⋯⋯⋯⋯⋯⋯ ○
☆ ⋯⋯⋯⋯⋯⋯⋯⋯ ○
☆ ⋯⋯⋯⋯⋯⋯⋯⋯ ○
☆ ⋯⋯⋯⋯⋯⋯⋯⋯ ○
☆ ⋯⋯⋯⋯⋯⋯⋯⋯ ○

Maintenance
☆ ⋯⋯⋯⋯⋯⋯⋯⋯ ○
☆ ⋯⋯⋯⋯⋯⋯⋯⋯ ○
☆ ⋯⋯⋯⋯⋯⋯⋯⋯ ○
☆ ⋯⋯⋯⋯⋯⋯⋯⋯ ○
☆ ⋯⋯⋯⋯⋯⋯⋯⋯ ○
☆ ⋯⋯⋯⋯⋯⋯⋯⋯ ○

Pest Control
☆ ⋯⋯⋯⋯⋯⋯⋯⋯ ○
☆ ⋯⋯⋯⋯⋯⋯⋯⋯ ○
☆ ⋯⋯⋯⋯⋯⋯⋯⋯ ○
☆ ⋯⋯⋯⋯⋯⋯⋯⋯ ○
☆ ⋯⋯⋯⋯⋯⋯⋯⋯ ○
☆ ⋯⋯⋯⋯⋯⋯⋯⋯ ○

Other
☆ ⋯⋯⋯⋯⋯⋯⋯⋯ ○
☆ ⋯⋯⋯⋯⋯⋯⋯⋯ ○
☆ ⋯⋯⋯⋯⋯⋯⋯⋯ ○
☆ ⋯⋯⋯⋯⋯⋯⋯⋯ ○
☆ ⋯⋯⋯⋯⋯⋯⋯⋯ ○
☆ ⋯⋯⋯⋯⋯⋯⋯⋯ ○

Purchasing | Cost

Harvesting | Amount

Weekly Journal

MONTH

Week 4

Start Date

Weather

Wildlife

Blooms

Highlight

MONTH

Week 5

Start Date

Weather

Wildlife

Blooms

Highlight

Things to Do

Planting
☆ _____ ○
☆ _____ ○
☆ _____ ○
☆ _____ ○
☆ _____ ○
☆ _____ ○

Propagation
☆ _____ ○
☆ _____ ○
☆ _____ ○
☆ _____ ○
☆ _____ ○
☆ _____ ○

Pruning
☆ _____ ○
☆ _____ ○
☆ _____ ○
☆ _____ ○
☆ _____ ○
☆ _____ ○

Maintenance
☆ _____ ○
☆ _____ ○
☆ _____ ○
☆ _____ ○
☆ _____ ○
☆ _____ ○

Pest Control
☆ _____ ○
☆ _____ ○
☆ _____ ○
☆ _____ ○
☆ _____ ○
☆ _____ ○

Other
☆ _____ ○
☆ _____ ○
☆ _____ ○
☆ _____ ○
☆ _____ ○
☆ _____ ○

Purchasing	Cost

Harvesting	Amount

Weekly Journal

Monthly Roundup

Use this space to affix photographs or make sketches of your garden as is looks now.

Jobs this Month

- ○ ....
- ○ ....
- ○ ....
- ○ ....
- ○ ....
- ○ ....
- ○ ....
- ○ ....
- ○ ....
- ○ ....
- ○ ....
- ○ ....
- ○ ....

MONTH

Week 1

Start Date

Weather

Wildlife

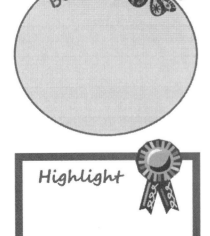

Blooms

Highlight

Things to Do

Planting
☆ ○
☆ ○
☆ ○
☆ ○
☆ ○
☆ ○

Propagation
☆ ○
☆ ○
☆ ○
☆ ○
☆ ○
☆ ○

Pruning
☆ ○
☆ ○
☆ ○
☆ ○
☆ ○
☆ ○

Maintenance
☆ ○
☆ ○
☆ ○
☆ ○
☆ ○
☆ ○

Pest Control
☆ ○
☆ ○
☆ ○
☆ ○
☆ ○
☆ ○

Other
☆ ○
☆ ○
☆ ○
☆ ○
☆ ○
☆ ○

Purchasing	Cost

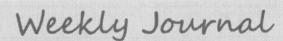

Harvesting	Amount

Weekly Journal

Things to Do

Planting
☆ _____ ○
☆ _____ ○
☆ _____ ○
☆ _____ ○
☆ _____ ○
☆ _____ ○

Propagation
☆ _____ ○
☆ _____ ○
☆ _____ ○
☆ _____ ○
☆ _____ ○
☆ _____ ○

Pruning
☆ _____ ○
☆ _____ ○
☆ _____ ○
☆ _____ ○
☆ _____ ○
☆ _____ ○

Maintenance
☆ _____ ○
☆ _____ ○
☆ _____ ○
☆ _____ ○
☆ _____ ○
☆ _____ ○

Pest Control
☆ _____ ○
☆ _____ ○
☆ _____ ○
☆ _____ ○
☆ _____ ○
☆ _____ ○

Other
☆ _____ ○
☆ _____ ○
☆ _____ ○
☆ _____ ○
☆ _____ ○
☆ _____ ○

Purchasing | Cost
_____
_____
_____
_____
_____

Harvesting | Amount
_____
_____
_____
_____
_____

Weekly Journal

MONTH

Week 2

Start Date

Weather

Wildlife

Blooms

Highlight

MONTH

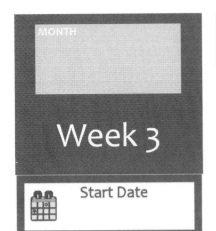

MONTH

Week 3

Start Date

Weather

Wildlife

Blooms

Highlight

Things to Do

Planting	Propagation	Pruning
☆ ○	☆ ○	☆ ○
☆ ○	☆ ○	☆ ○
☆ ○	☆ ○	☆ ○
☆ ○	☆ ○	☆ ○
☆ ○	☆ ○	☆ ○
☆ ○	☆ ○	☆ ○

Maintenance	Pest Control	Other
☆ ○	☆ ○	☆ ○
☆ ○	☆ ○	☆ ○
☆ ○	☆ ○	☆ ○
☆ ○	☆ ○	☆ ○
☆ ○	☆ ○	☆ ○
☆ ○	☆ ○	☆ ○

Purchasing	Cost

Harvesting	Amount

Weekly Journal

Things to Do

Planting
☆ _____ ○
☆ _____ ○
☆ _____ ○
☆ _____ ○
☆ _____ ○
☆ _____ ○

Propagation
☆ _____ ○
☆ _____ ○
☆ _____ ○
☆ _____ ○
☆ _____ ○
☆ _____ ○

Pruning
☆ _____ ○
☆ _____ ○
☆ _____ ○
☆ _____ ○
☆ _____ ○
☆ _____ ○

Maintenance
☆ _____ ○
☆ _____ ○
☆ _____ ○
☆ _____ ○
☆ _____ ○
☆ _____ ○

Pest Control
☆ _____ ○
☆ _____ ○
☆ _____ ○
☆ _____ ○
☆ _____ ○
☆ _____ ○

Other
☆ _____ ○
☆ _____ ○
☆ _____ ○
☆ _____ ○
☆ _____ ○
☆ _____ ○

Purchasing	Cost

Harvesting	Amount

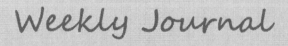

Weekly Journal

MONTH

Week 4

Start Date

Weather

Wildlife

Blooms

Highlight

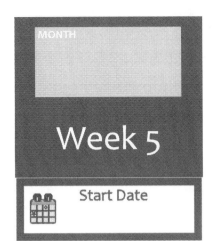

MONTH

Week 5

Start Date

Weather

Wildlife

Blooms

Highlight

Things to Do

Planting
☆ ○
☆ ○
☆ ○
☆ ○
☆ ○
☆ ○

Propagation
☆ ○
☆ ○
☆ ○
☆ ○
☆ ○
☆ ○

Pruning
☆ ○
☆ ○
☆ ○
☆ ○
☆ ○
☆ ○

Maintenance
☆ ○
☆ ○
☆ ○
☆ ○
☆ ○
☆ ○

Pest Control
☆ ○
☆ ○
☆ ○
☆ ○
☆ ○
☆ ○

Other
☆ ○
☆ ○
☆ ○
☆ ○
☆ ○
☆ ○

Purchasing
Cost

Harvesting
Amount

Weekly Journal

Monthly Roundup

Use this space to affix photographs or make sketches of your garden as is looks now.

Jobs this Month

○ ....
○ ....
○ ....
○ ....
○ ....
○ ....
○ ....
○ ....
○ ....
○ ....
○ ....

MONTH

Week 1

Start Date

Weather

Wildlife

Blooms

Highlight

Things to Do

Planting
☆ _____ ○
☆ _____ ○
☆ _____ ○
☆ _____ ○
☆ _____ ○
☆ _____ ○

Propagation
☆ _____ ○
☆ _____ ○
☆ _____ ○
☆ _____ ○
☆ _____ ○
☆ _____ ○

Pruning
☆ _____ ○
☆ _____ ○
☆ _____ ○
☆ _____ ○
☆ _____ ○
☆ _____ ○

Maintenance
☆ _____ ○
☆ _____ ○
☆ _____ ○
☆ _____ ○
☆ _____ ○
☆ _____ ○

Pest Control
☆ _____ ○
☆ _____ ○
☆ _____ ○
☆ _____ ○
☆ _____ ○
☆ _____ ○

Other
☆ _____ ○
☆ _____ ○
☆ _____ ○
☆ _____ ○
☆ _____ ○
☆ _____ ○

Purchasing	Cost

Harvesting	Amount

Weekly Journal

Things to Do

Week 2

Start Date

Planting
☆ .... ○
☆ .... ○
☆ .... ○
☆ .... ○
☆ .... ○
☆ .... ○

Propagation
☆ .... ○
☆ .... ○
☆ .... ○
☆ .... ○
☆ .... ○
☆ .... ○

Pruning
☆ .... ○
☆ .... ○
☆ .... ○
☆ .... ○
☆ .... ○
☆ .... ○

Maintenance
☆ .... ○
☆ .... ○
☆ .... ○
☆ .... ○
☆ .... ○
☆ .... ○

Pest Control
☆ .... ○
☆ .... ○
☆ .... ○
☆ .... ○
☆ .... ○
☆ .... ○

Other
☆ .... ○
☆ .... ○
☆ .... ○
☆ .... ○
☆ .... ○
☆ .... ○

Purchasing	Cost

Harvesting	Amount

Weather

Wildlife

Blooms

Highlight

Weekly Journal

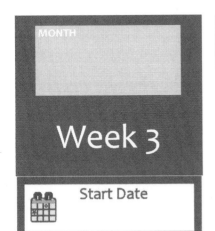

MONTH

Week 3

Start Date

Weather

Wildlife

Blooms

Highlight

Things to Do

Planting
☆ ○
☆ ○
☆ ○
☆ ○
☆ ○
☆ ○

Propagation
☆ ○
☆ ○
☆ ○
☆ ○
☆ ○
☆ ○

Pruning
☆ ○
☆ ○
☆ ○
☆ ○
☆ ○
☆ ○

Maintenance
☆ ○
☆ ○
☆ ○
☆ ○
☆ ○
☆ ○

Pest Control
☆ ○
☆ ○
☆ ○
☆ ○
☆ ○
☆ ○

Other
☆ ○
☆ ○
☆ ○
☆ ○
☆ ○
☆ ○

Purchasing	Cost

Harvesting	Amount

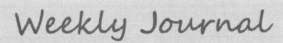

Weekly Journal

Things to Do

Planting
☆ _____ ○
☆ _____ ○
☆ _____ ○
☆ _____ ○
☆ _____ ○
☆ _____ ○

Propagation
☆ _____ ○
☆ _____ ○
☆ _____ ○
☆ _____ ○
☆ _____ ○
☆ _____ ○

Pruning
☆ _____ ○
☆ _____ ○
☆ _____ ○
☆ _____ ○
☆ _____ ○
☆ _____ ○

Maintenance
☆ _____ ○
☆ _____ ○
☆ _____ ○
☆ _____ ○
☆ _____ ○
☆ _____ ○

Pest Control
☆ _____ ○
☆ _____ ○
☆ _____ ○
☆ _____ ○
☆ _____ ○
☆ _____ ○

Other
☆ _____ ○
☆ _____ ○
☆ _____ ○
☆ _____ ○
☆ _____ ○
☆ _____ ○

Purchasing	Cost

Harvesting	Amount

Weekly Journal

MONTH

Week 4

Start Date

Weather

Wildlife

Blooms

Highlight

MONTH

Week 5

Start Date

Weather

Wildlife

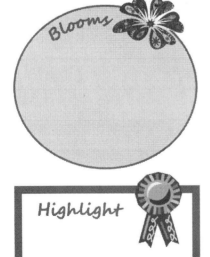

Blooms

Highlight

Things to Do

Planting
☆ ○
☆ ○
☆ ○
☆ ○
☆ ○
☆ ○

Propagation
☆ ○
☆ ○
☆ ○
☆ ○
☆ ○
☆ ○

Pruning
☆ ○
☆ ○
☆ ○
☆ ○
☆ ○
☆ ○

Maintenance
☆ ○
☆ ○
☆ ○
☆ ○
☆ ○
☆ ○

Pest Control
☆ ○
☆ ○
☆ ○
☆ ○
☆ ○
☆ ○

Other
☆ ○
☆ ○
☆ ○
☆ ○
☆ ○
☆ ○

Purchasing	Cost

Harvesting	Amount

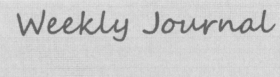

Weekly Journal

Monthly Roundup

Use this space to affix photographs or make sketches of your garden as is looks now.

Jobs this Month

- ○
- ○
- ○
- ○
- ○
- ○
- ○
- ○
- ○
- ○
- ○
- ○

MONTH

Week 1

Start Date

Weather

Wildlife

Blooms

Highlight

Things to Do

Planting
☆ ○
☆ ○
☆ ○
☆ ○
☆ ○
☆ ○

Propagation
☆ ○
☆ ○
☆ ○
☆ ○
☆ ○
☆ ○

Pruning
☆ ○
☆ ○
☆ ○
☆ ○
☆ ○
☆ ○

Maintenance
☆ ○
☆ ○
☆ ○
☆ ○
☆ ○
☆ ○

Pest Control
☆ ○
☆ ○
☆ ○
☆ ○
☆ ○
☆ ○

Other
☆ ○
☆ ○
☆ ○
☆ ○
☆ ○
☆ ○

Purchasing	Cost

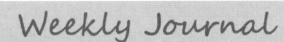

Harvesting	Amount

Weekly Journal

Things to Do

Planting
☆ ○
☆ ○
☆ ○
☆ ○
☆ ○
☆ ○

Propagation
☆ ○
☆ ○
☆ ○
☆ ○
☆ ○
☆ ○

Pruning
☆ ○
☆ ○
☆ ○
☆ ○
☆ ○
☆ ○

Maintenance
☆ ○
☆ ○
☆ ○
☆ ○
☆ ○
☆ ○

Pest Control
☆ ○
☆ ○
☆ ○
☆ ○
☆ ○
☆ ○

Other
☆ ○
☆ ○
☆ ○
☆ ○
☆ ○
☆ ○

Purchasing	Cost

Harvesting	Amount

Weekly Journal

Week 2

Start Date

Weather

Wildlife

Blooms

Highlight

MONTH

Week 3

Start Date

Weather

Wildlife

Blooms

Highlight

Things to Do

Planting
☆ _____ ○
☆ _____ ○
☆ _____ ○
☆ _____ ○
☆ _____ ○
☆ _____ ○

Propagation
☆ _____ ○
☆ _____ ○
☆ _____ ○
☆ _____ ○
☆ _____ ○
☆ _____ ○

Pruning
☆ _____ ○
☆ _____ ○
☆ _____ ○
☆ _____ ○
☆ _____ ○

Maintenance
☆ _____ ○
☆ _____ ○
☆ _____ ○
☆ _____ ○
☆ _____ ○

Pest Control
☆ _____ ○
☆ _____ ○
☆ _____ ○
☆ _____ ○
☆ _____ ○

Other
☆ _____ ○
☆ _____ ○
☆ _____ ○
☆ _____ ○
☆ _____ ○

Purchasing	Cost

Harvesting	Amount

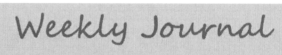

Weekly Journal

Things to Do

Planting
☆ ○
☆ ○
☆ ○
☆ ○
☆ ○
☆ ○

Propagation
☆ ○
☆ ○
☆ ○
☆ ○
☆ ○
☆ ○

Pruning
☆ ○
☆ ○
☆ ○
☆ ○
☆ ○
☆ ○

Maintenance
☆ ○
☆ ○
☆ ○
☆ ○
☆ ○
☆ ○

Pest Control
☆ ○
☆ ○
☆ ○
☆ ○
☆ ○
☆ ○

Other
☆ ○
☆ ○
☆ ○
☆ ○
☆ ○
☆ ○

Purchasing	Cost

Harvesting	Amount

Weekly Journal

MONTH

Week 4

Start Date

Weather

Wildlife

Blooms

Highlight

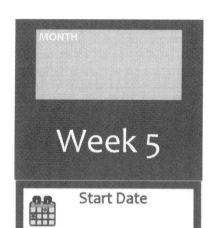

MONTH

Week 5

Start Date

Weather

Wildlife

Blooms

Highlight

Things to Do

Planting
☆ _____ ○
☆ _____ ○
☆ _____ ○
☆ _____ ○
☆ _____ ○
☆ _____ ○

Propagation
☆ _____ ○
☆ _____ ○
☆ _____ ○
☆ _____ ○
☆ _____ ○
☆ _____ ○

Pruning
☆ _____ ○
☆ _____ ○
☆ _____ ○
☆ _____ ○
☆ _____ ○
☆ _____ ○

Maintenance
☆ _____ ○
☆ _____ ○
☆ _____ ○
☆ _____ ○
☆ _____ ○
☆ _____ ○

Pest Control
☆ _____ ○
☆ _____ ○
☆ _____ ○
☆ _____ ○
☆ _____ ○
☆ _____ ○

Other
☆ _____ ○
☆ _____ ○
☆ _____ ○
☆ _____ ○
☆ _____ ○
☆ _____ ○

Purchasing	Cost

Harvesting	Amount

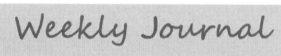

Weekly Journal

Monthly Roundup

Use this space to affix photographs or make sketches of your garden as is looks now.

Jobs this Month

- ◯
- ◯
- ◯
- ◯
- ◯
- ◯
- ◯
- ◯
- ◯
- ◯
- ◯
- ◯
- ◯

MONTH

Week 1

Start Date

Weather

Wildlife

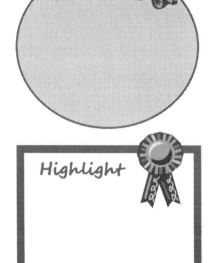

Blooms

Highlight

Things to Do

Planting
☆ _____ ○
☆ _____ ○
☆ _____ ○
☆ _____ ○
☆ _____ ○
☆ _____ ○

Propagation
☆ _____ ○
☆ _____ ○
☆ _____ ○
☆ _____ ○
☆ _____ ○
☆ _____ ○

Pruning
☆ _____ ○
☆ _____ ○
☆ _____ ○
☆ _____ ○
☆ _____ ○
☆ _____ ○

Maintenance
☆ _____ ○
☆ _____ ○
☆ _____ ○
☆ _____ ○
☆ _____ ○
☆ _____ ○

Pest Control
☆ _____ ○
☆ _____ ○
☆ _____ ○
☆ _____ ○
☆ _____ ○
☆ _____ ○

Other
☆ _____ ○
☆ _____ ○
☆ _____ ○
☆ _____ ○
☆ _____ ○
☆ _____ ○

Purchasing   Cost

Harvesting   Amount

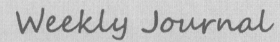

Weekly Journal

Things to Do

Planting
☆ _____ ○
☆ _____ ○
☆ _____ ○
☆ _____ ○
☆ _____ ○
☆ _____ ○

Propagation
☆ _____ ○
☆ _____ ○
☆ _____ ○
☆ _____ ○
☆ _____ ○
☆ _____ ○

Pruning
☆ _____ ○
☆ _____ ○
☆ _____ ○
☆ _____ ○
☆ _____ ○
☆ _____ ○

Maintenance
☆ _____ ○
☆ _____ ○
☆ _____ ○
☆ _____ ○
☆ _____ ○

Pest Control
☆ _____ ○
☆ _____ ○
☆ _____ ○
☆ _____ ○
☆ _____ ○

Other
☆ _____ ○
☆ _____ ○
☆ _____ ○
☆ _____ ○
☆ _____ ○

Purchasing   Cost

Harvesting   Amount

Weekly Journal

MONTH

Week 2

📅 Start Date

Weather

Wildlife

Blooms

Highlight

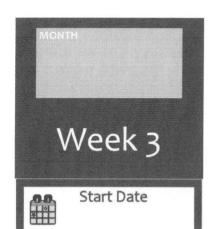

MONTH

Week 3

Start Date

Weather

Wildlife

Blooms

Highlight

Things to Do

Planting
☆ _____ ○
☆ _____ ○
☆ _____ ○
☆ _____ ○
☆ _____ ○
☆ _____ ○

Propagation
☆ _____ ○
☆ _____ ○
☆ _____ ○
☆ _____ ○
☆ _____ ○
☆ _____ ○

Pruning
☆ _____ ○
☆ _____ ○
☆ _____ ○
☆ _____ ○
☆ _____ ○
☆ _____ ○

Maintenance
☆ _____ ○
☆ _____ ○
☆ _____ ○
☆ _____ ○
☆ _____ ○
☆ _____ ○

Pest Control
☆ _____ ○
☆ _____ ○
☆ _____ ○
☆ _____ ○
☆ _____ ○
☆ _____ ○

Other
☆ _____ ○
☆ _____ ○
☆ _____ ○
☆ _____ ○
☆ _____ ○
☆ _____ ○

Purchasing   Cost

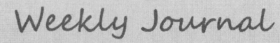

Harvesting   Amount

Weekly Journal

Things to Do

Planting
☆ .... ○
☆ .... ○
☆ .... ○
☆ .... ○
☆ .... ○
☆ .... ○

Propagation
☆ .... ○
☆ .... ○
☆ .... ○
☆ .... ○
☆ .... ○
☆ .... ○

Pruning
☆ .... ○
☆ .... ○
☆ .... ○
☆ .... ○
☆ .... ○
☆ .... ○

Maintenance
☆ .... ○
☆ .... ○
☆ .... ○
☆ .... ○
☆ .... ○
☆ .... ○

Pest Control
☆ .... ○
☆ .... ○
☆ .... ○
☆ .... ○
☆ .... ○
☆ .... ○

Other
☆ .... ○
☆ .... ○
☆ .... ○
☆ .... ○
☆ .... ○
☆ .... ○

Purchasing | Cost

Harvesting | Amount

Weekly Journal

MONTH

Week 4

Start Date

Weather

Wildlife

Blooms

Highlight

MONTH

Week 5

📅 **Start Date**

Weather

Wildlife

Blooms

Highlight

Things to Do

Planting
☆ .... ○
☆ .... ○
☆ .... ○
☆ .... ○
☆ .... ○
☆ .... ○

Propagation
☆ .... ○
☆ .... ○
☆ .... ○
☆ .... ○
☆ .... ○
☆ .... ○

Pruning
☆ .... ○
☆ .... ○
☆ .... ○
☆ .... ○
☆ .... ○
☆ .... ○

Maintenance
☆ .... ○
☆ .... ○
☆ .... ○
☆ .... ○
☆ .... ○
☆ .... ○

Pest Control
☆ .... ○
☆ .... ○
☆ .... ○
☆ .... ○
☆ .... ○
☆ .... ○

Other
☆ .... ○
☆ .... ○
☆ .... ○
☆ .... ○
☆ .... ○
☆ .... ○

Purchasing	Cost

Harvesting	Amount

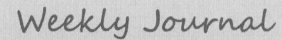

Weekly Journal

Monthly Roundup

Use this space to affix photographs or make sketches of your garden as is looks now.

Jobs this Month

- ○
- ○
- ○
- ○
- ○
- ○
- ○
- ○
- ○
- ○
- ○
- ○
- ○

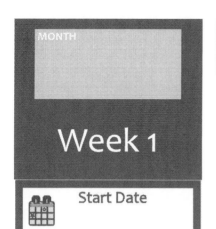

MONTH

Week 1

Start Date

Weather

Wildlife

Blooms

Highlight

Things to Do

Planting
☆ _____ ○
☆ _____ ○
☆ _____ ○
☆ _____ ○
☆ _____ ○
☆ _____ ○

Propagation
☆ _____ ○
☆ _____ ○
☆ _____ ○
☆ _____ ○
☆ _____ ○
☆ _____ ○

Pruning
☆ _____ ○
☆ _____ ○
☆ _____ ○
☆ _____ ○
☆ _____ ○
☆ _____ ○

Maintenance
☆ _____ ○
☆ _____ ○
☆ _____ ○
☆ _____ ○
☆ _____ ○
☆ _____ ○

Pest Control
☆ _____ ○
☆ _____ ○
☆ _____ ○
☆ _____ ○
☆ _____ ○
☆ _____ ○

Other
☆ _____ ○
☆ _____ ○
☆ _____ ○
☆ _____ ○
☆ _____ ○
☆ _____ ○

Purchasing	Cost

Harvesting	Amount

Weekly Journal

Things to Do

Planting
☆ _____ ○
☆ _____ ○
☆ _____ ○
☆ _____ ○
☆ _____ ○
☆ _____ ○

Propagation
☆ _____ ○
☆ _____ ○
☆ _____ ○
☆ _____ ○
☆ _____ ○
☆ _____ ○

Pruning
☆ _____ ○
☆ _____ ○
☆ _____ ○
☆ _____ ○
☆ _____ ○
☆ _____ ○

Maintenance
☆ _____ ○
☆ _____ ○
☆ _____ ○
☆ _____ ○
☆ _____ ○
☆ _____ ○

Pest Control
☆ _____ ○
☆ _____ ○
☆ _____ ○
☆ _____ ○
☆ _____ ○
☆ _____ ○

Other
☆ _____ ○
☆ _____ ○
☆ _____ ○
☆ _____ ○
☆ _____ ○
☆ _____ ○

Purchasing   Cost
_____
_____
_____
_____
_____

Harvesting   Amount
_____
_____
_____
_____
_____

Weekly Journal

MONTH

Week 2

Start Date

Weather

Wildlife

Blooms

Highlight

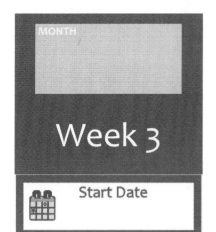

MONTH

Week 3

Start Date

Weather

Wildlife

Blooms

Highlight

Things to Do

Planting
☆ ○
☆ ○
☆ ○
☆ ○
☆ ○
☆ ○

Propagation
☆ ○
☆ ○
☆ ○
☆ ○
☆ ○
☆ ○

Pruning
☆ ○
☆ ○
☆ ○
☆ ○
☆ ○
☆ ○

Maintenance
☆ ○
☆ ○
☆ ○
☆ ○
☆ ○
☆ ○

Pest Control
☆ ○
☆ ○
☆ ○
☆ ○
☆ ○
☆ ○

Other
☆ ○
☆ ○
☆ ○
☆ ○
☆ ○
☆ ○

Purchasing	Cost

Harvesting	Amount

Weekly Journal

Things to Do

Planting
☆ .... ○
☆ .... ○
☆ .... ○
☆ .... ○
☆ .... ○
☆ .... ○

Propagation
☆ .... ○
☆ .... ○
☆ .... ○
☆ .... ○
☆ .... ○
☆ .... ○

Pruning
☆ .... ○
☆ .... ○
☆ .... ○
☆ .... ○
☆ .... ○
☆ .... ○

Maintenance
☆ .... ○
☆ .... ○
☆ .... ○
☆ .... ○
☆ .... ○
☆ .... ○

Pest Control
☆ .... ○
☆ .... ○
☆ .... ○
☆ .... ○
☆ .... ○
☆ .... ○

Other
☆ .... ○
☆ .... ○
☆ .... ○
☆ .... ○
☆ .... ○
☆ .... ○

Purchasing | Cost

Harvesting | Amount

Weekly Journal

MONTH

Week 4

Start Date

Weather

Wildlife

Blooms

Highlight

MONTH

Week 5

Start Date

Weather

Wildlife

Blooms

Highlight

Things to Do

Planting
☆ _____ ○
☆ _____ ○
☆ _____ ○
☆ _____ ○
☆ _____ ○
☆ _____ ○

Propagation
☆ _____ ○
☆ _____ ○
☆ _____ ○
☆ _____ ○
☆ _____ ○
☆ _____ ○

Pruning
☆ _____ ○
☆ _____ ○
☆ _____ ○
☆ _____ ○
☆ _____ ○
☆ _____ ○

Maintenance
☆ _____ ○
☆ _____ ○
☆ _____ ○
☆ _____ ○
☆ _____ ○
☆ _____ ○

Pest Control
☆ _____ ○
☆ _____ ○
☆ _____ ○
☆ _____ ○
☆ _____ ○
☆ _____ ○

Other
☆ _____ ○
☆ _____ ○
☆ _____ ○
☆ _____ ○
☆ _____ ○
☆ _____ ○

Purchasing	Cost

Harvesting	Amount

Weekly Journal

Monthly Roundup

Use this space to affix photographs or make sketches of your garden as is looks now.

Jobs this Month

- ○
- ○
- ○
- ○
- ○
- ○
- ○
- ○
- ○
- ○
- ○

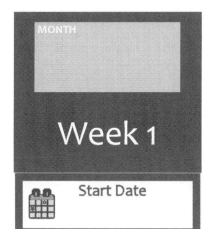

MONTH

Week 1

Start Date

Weather

Wildlife

Blooms

Highlight

Things to Do

Planting
☆ ⚪
☆ ⚪
☆ ⚪
☆ ⚪
☆ ⚪
☆ ⚪

Propagation
☆ ⚪
☆ ⚪
☆ ⚪
☆ ⚪
☆ ⚪
☆ ⚪

Pruning
☆ ⚪
☆ ⚪
☆ ⚪
☆ ⚪
☆ ⚪
☆ ⚪

Maintenance
☆ ⚪
☆ ⚪
☆ ⚪
☆ ⚪
☆ ⚪
☆ ⚪

Pest Control
☆ ⚪
☆ ⚪
☆ ⚪
☆ ⚪
☆ ⚪
☆ ⚪

Other
☆ ⚪
☆ ⚪
☆ ⚪
☆ ⚪
☆ ⚪
☆ ⚪

Purchasing | Cost

Harvesting | Amount

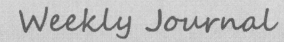

Weekly Journal

Things to Do

Planting
☆ _____ ○
☆ _____ ○
☆ _____ ○
☆ _____ ○
☆ _____ ○
☆ _____ ○

Propagation
☆ _____ ○
☆ _____ ○
☆ _____ ○
☆ _____ ○
☆ _____ ○
☆ _____ ○

Pruning
☆ _____ ○
☆ _____ ○
☆ _____ ○
☆ _____ ○
☆ _____ ○
☆ _____ ○

Maintenance
☆ _____ ○
☆ _____ ○
☆ _____ ○
☆ _____ ○
☆ _____ ○
☆ _____ ○

Pest Control
☆ _____ ○
☆ _____ ○
☆ _____ ○
☆ _____ ○
☆ _____ ○
☆ _____ ○

Other
☆ _____ ○
☆ _____ ○
☆ _____ ○
☆ _____ ○
☆ _____ ○
☆ _____ ○

Purchasing | Cost
_____
_____
_____
_____
_____

Harvesting | Amount
_____
_____
_____
_____
_____

Weekly Journal

MONTH

Week 2

Start Date

Weather

Wildlife

Blooms

Highlight

MONTH

Week 3

Start Date

Weather

Wildlife

Blooms

Highlight

Things to Do

Planting
☆ _____ ○
☆ _____ ○
☆ _____ ○
☆ _____ ○
☆ _____ ○
☆ _____ ○

Propagation
☆ _____ ○
☆ _____ ○
☆ _____ ○
☆ _____ ○
☆ _____ ○
☆ _____ ○

Pruning
☆ _____ ○
☆ _____ ○
☆ _____ ○
☆ _____ ○
☆ _____ ○
☆ _____ ○

Maintenance
☆ _____ ○
☆ _____ ○
☆ _____ ○
☆ _____ ○
☆ _____ ○
☆ _____ ○

Pest Control
☆ _____ ○
☆ _____ ○
☆ _____ ○
☆ _____ ○
☆ _____ ○
☆ _____ ○

Other
☆ _____ ○
☆ _____ ○
☆ _____ ○
☆ _____ ○
☆ _____ ○
☆ _____ ○

Purchasing	Cost

Harvesting	Amount

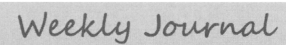

Weekly Journal

Things to Do

Planting
☆ _____ ○
☆ _____ ○
☆ _____ ○
☆ _____ ○
☆ _____ ○
☆ _____ ○

Propagation
☆ _____ ○
☆ _____ ○
☆ _____ ○
☆ _____ ○
☆ _____ ○
☆ _____ ○

Pruning
☆ _____ ○
☆ _____ ○
☆ _____ ○
☆ _____ ○
☆ _____ ○
☆ _____ ○

Maintenance
☆ _____ ○
☆ _____ ○
☆ _____ ○
☆ _____ ○
☆ _____ ○
☆ _____ ○

Pest Control
☆ _____ ○
☆ _____ ○
☆ _____ ○
☆ _____ ○
☆ _____ ○
☆ _____ ○

Other
☆ _____ ○
☆ _____ ○
☆ _____ ○
☆ _____ ○
☆ _____ ○
☆ _____ ○

Purchasing — Cost

Harvesting — Amount

Weekly Journal

MONTH

Week 4

Start Date

Weather

Wildlife

Blooms

Highlight

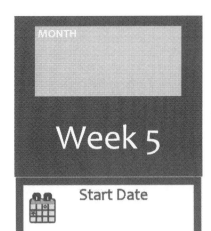

MONTH

Week 5

Start Date

Weather

Wildlife

Blooms

Highlight

Things to Do

Planting
☆ ──────────── ○
☆ ──────────── ○
☆ ──────────── ○
☆ ──────────── ○
☆ ──────────── ○
☆ ──────────── ○

Propagation
☆ ──────────── ○
☆ ──────────── ○
☆ ──────────── ○
☆ ──────────── ○
☆ ──────────── ○
☆ ──────────── ○

Pruning
☆ ──────────── ○
☆ ──────────── ○
☆ ──────────── ○
☆ ──────────── ○
☆ ──────────── ○
☆ ──────────── ○

Maintenance
☆ ──────────── ○
☆ ──────────── ○
☆ ──────────── ○
☆ ──────────── ○
☆ ──────────── ○
☆ ──────────── ○

Pest Control
☆ ──────────── ○
☆ ──────────── ○
☆ ──────────── ○
☆ ──────────── ○
☆ ──────────── ○
☆ ──────────── ○

Other
☆ ──────────── ○
☆ ──────────── ○
☆ ──────────── ○
☆ ──────────── ○
☆ ──────────── ○
☆ ──────────── ○

Purchasing	Cost

Harvesting	Amount

Weekly Journal

Monthly Roundup

Use this space to affix photographs or make sketches of your garden as is looks now.

Jobs this Month

○ _____
_____

○ _____
_____

○ _____
_____

○ _____
_____

○ _____
_____

○ _____
_____

○ _____
_____

○ _____
_____

○ _____
_____

○ _____
_____

○ _____
_____

○ _____
_____

MONTH

Week 1

Start Date

Weather

Wildlife

Blooms

Highlight

Things to Do

Planting
☆ _____ ○
☆ _____ ○
☆ _____ ○
☆ _____ ○
☆ _____ ○
☆ _____ ○

Propagation
☆ _____ ○
☆ _____ ○
☆ _____ ○
☆ _____ ○
☆ _____ ○
☆ _____ ○

Pruning
☆ _____ ○
☆ _____ ○
☆ _____ ○
☆ _____ ○
☆ _____ ○
☆ _____ ○

Maintenance
☆ _____ ○
☆ _____ ○
☆ _____ ○
☆ _____ ○
☆ _____ ○
☆ _____ ○

Pest Control
☆ _____ ○
☆ _____ ○
☆ _____ ○
☆ _____ ○
☆ _____ ○
☆ _____ ○

Other
☆ _____ ○
☆ _____ ○
☆ _____ ○
☆ _____ ○
☆ _____ ○
☆ _____ ○

Purchasing	Cost

Harvesting	Amount

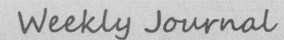

Weekly Journal

Things to Do

Planting
☆ _____ ○
☆ _____ ○
☆ _____ ○
☆ _____ ○
☆ _____ ○
☆ _____ ○

Propagation
☆ _____ ○
☆ _____ ○
☆ _____ ○
☆ _____ ○
☆ _____ ○
☆ _____ ○

Pruning
☆ _____ ○
☆ _____ ○
☆ _____ ○
☆ _____ ○
☆ _____ ○
☆ _____ ○

Maintenance
☆ _____ ○
☆ _____ ○
☆ _____ ○
☆ _____ ○
☆ _____ ○

Pest Control
☆ _____ ○
☆ _____ ○
☆ _____ ○
☆ _____ ○
☆ _____ ○

Other
☆ _____ ○
☆ _____ ○
☆ _____ ○
☆ _____ ○
☆ _____ ○

Purchasing   Cost
_____
_____
_____
_____
_____

Harvesting   Amount
_____
_____
_____
_____
_____

Weekly Journal

MONTH

Week 2

Start Date

Weather

Wildlife

Blooms

Highlight

MONTH

Week 3

Start Date

Weather

Wildlife

Blooms

Highlight

Things to Do

Planting
☆ .... ○
☆ .... ○
☆ .... ○
☆ .... ○
☆ .... ○
☆ .... ○

Propagation
☆ .... ○
☆ .... ○
☆ .... ○
☆ .... ○
☆ .... ○
☆ .... ○

Pruning
☆ .... ○
☆ .... ○
☆ .... ○
☆ .... ○
☆ .... ○
☆ .... ○

Maintenance
☆ .... ○
☆ .... ○
☆ .... ○
☆ .... ○
☆ .... ○
☆ .... ○

Pest Control
☆ .... ○
☆ .... ○
☆ .... ○
☆ .... ○
☆ .... ○
☆ .... ○

Other
☆ .... ○
☆ .... ○
☆ .... ○
☆ .... ○
☆ .... ○
☆ .... ○

Purchasing	Cost

Harvesting	Amount

Weekly Journal

Things to Do

Planting
☆ _____ ○
☆ _____ ○
☆ _____ ○
☆ _____ ○
☆ _____ ○
☆ _____ ○

Propagation
☆ _____ ○
☆ _____ ○
☆ _____ ○
☆ _____ ○
☆ _____ ○
☆ _____ ○

Pruning
☆ _____ ○
☆ _____ ○
☆ _____ ○
☆ _____ ○
☆ _____ ○
☆ _____ ○

Maintenance
☆ _____ ○
☆ _____ ○
☆ _____ ○
☆ _____ ○
☆ _____ ○
☆ _____ ○

Pest Control
☆ _____ ○
☆ _____ ○
☆ _____ ○
☆ _____ ○
☆ _____ ○
☆ _____ ○

Other
☆ _____ ○
☆ _____ ○
☆ _____ ○
☆ _____ ○
☆ _____ ○
☆ _____ ○

Purchasing	Cost

Harvesting	Amount

Weekly Journal

MONTH

Week 4

Start Date

Weather

Wildlife

Blooms

Highlight

Week 5

Start Date

Weather

Wildlife

Blooms

Highlight

Things to Do

Planting
☆ ○
☆ ○
☆ ○
☆ ○
☆ ○
☆ ○

Propagation
☆ ○
☆ ○
☆ ○
☆ ○
☆ ○
☆ ○

Pruning
☆ ○
☆ ○
☆ ○
☆ ○
☆ ○
☆ ○

Maintenance
☆ ○
☆ ○
☆ ○
☆ ○
☆ ○
☆ ○

Pest Control
☆ ○
☆ ○
☆ ○
☆ ○
☆ ○
☆ ○

Other
☆ ○
☆ ○
☆ ○
☆ ○
☆ ○
☆ ○

Purchasing   Cost

Harvesting   Amount

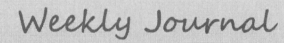

Weekly Journal

Monthly Roundup

Use this space to affix photographs or make sketches of your garden as is looks now.

Jobs this Month

○ _____
○ _____
○ _____
○ _____
○ _____
○ _____
○ _____
○ _____
○ _____
○ _____
○ _____
○ _____

MONTH

Week 1

Start Date

Weather

Wildlife

Blooms

Highlight

Things to Do

Planting
☆ _____ ○
☆ _____ ○
☆ _____ ○
☆ _____ ○
☆ _____ ○
☆ _____ ○

Propagation
☆ _____ ○
☆ _____ ○
☆ _____ ○
☆ _____ ○
☆ _____ ○
☆ _____ ○

Pruning
☆ _____ ○
☆ _____ ○
☆ _____ ○
☆ _____ ○
☆ _____ ○
☆ _____ ○

Maintenance
☆ _____ ○
☆ _____ ○
☆ _____ ○
☆ _____ ○
☆ _____ ○
☆ _____ ○

Pest Control
☆ _____ ○
☆ _____ ○
☆ _____ ○
☆ _____ ○
☆ _____ ○
☆ _____ ○

Other
☆ _____ ○
☆ _____ ○
☆ _____ ○
☆ _____ ○
☆ _____ ○
☆ _____ ○

Purchasing	Cost

Harvesting	Amount

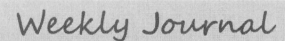

Weekly Journal

Things to Do

Planting
- ☆ ○
- ☆ ○
- ☆ ○
- ☆ ○
- ☆ ○
- ☆

Propagation
- ☆ ○
- ☆ ○
- ☆ ○
- ☆ ○
- ☆ ○
- ☆

Pruning
- ☆ ○
- ☆ ○
- ☆ ○
- ☆ ○
- ☆ ○
- ☆

Maintenance
- ☆ ○
- ☆ ○
- ☆ ○
- ☆ ○
- ☆ ○
- ☆ ○

Pest Control
- ☆ ○
- ☆ ○
- ☆ ○
- ☆ ○
- ☆ ○
- ☆ ○

Other
- ☆ ○
- ☆ ○
- ☆ ○
- ☆ ○
- ☆ ○
- ☆ ○

Purchasing | Cost

Harvesting | Amount

Weekly Journal

MONTH

Week 2

Start Date

Weather

Wildlife

Blooms

Highlight

MONTH

Week 3

Start Date

Weather

Wildlife

Blooms

Highlight

Things to Do

Planting
☆ ○
☆ ○
☆ ○
☆ ○
☆ ○
☆ ○

Propagation
☆ ○
☆ ○
☆ ○
☆ ○
☆ ○
☆ ○

Pruning
☆ ○
☆ ○
☆ ○
☆ ○
☆ ○
☆ ○

Maintenance
☆ ○
☆ ○
☆ ○
☆ ○
☆ ○
☆ ○

Pest Control
☆ ○
☆ ○
☆ ○
☆ ○
☆ ○
☆ ○

Other
☆ ○
☆ ○
☆ ○
☆ ○
☆ ○
☆ ○

Purchasing	Cost

Harvesting	Amount

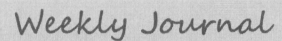

Weekly Journal

Things to Do

Planting
☆ _____ ○
☆ _____ ○
☆ _____ ○
☆ _____ ○
☆ _____ ○
☆ _____ ○

Propagation
☆ _____ ○
☆ _____ ○
☆ _____ ○
☆ _____ ○
☆ _____ ○
☆ _____ ○

Pruning
☆ _____ ○
☆ _____ ○
☆ _____ ○
☆ _____ ○
☆ _____ ○
☆ _____ ○

Maintenance
☆ _____ ○
☆ _____ ○
☆ _____ ○
☆ _____ ○
☆ _____ ○
☆ _____ ○

Pest Control
☆ _____ ○
☆ _____ ○
☆ _____ ○
☆ _____ ○
☆ _____ ○
☆ _____ ○

Other
☆ _____ ○
☆ _____ ○
☆ _____ ○
☆ _____ ○
☆ _____ ○
☆ _____ ○

Purchasing	Cost

Harvesting	Amount

Weekly Journal

MONTH

Week 4

Start Date

Weather

Wildlife

Blooms

Highlight

MONTH

Week 5

Start Date

Weather

Wildlife

Blooms

Highlight

Things to Do

Planting
☆ ○
☆ ○
☆ ○
☆ ○
☆ ○
☆ ○

Propagation
☆ ○
☆ ○
☆ ○
☆ ○
☆ ○
☆ ○

Pruning
☆ ○
☆ ○
☆ ○
☆ ○
☆ ○
☆ ○

Maintenance
☆ ○
☆ ○
☆ ○
☆ ○
☆ ○
☆ ○

Pest Control
☆ ○
☆ ○
☆ ○
☆ ○
☆ ○
☆ ○

Other
☆ ○
☆ ○
☆ ○
☆ ○
☆ ○
☆ ○

Purchasing	Cost

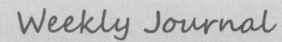

Harvesting	Amount

Weekly Journal

Monthly Roundup

Affix photographs or make sketches of your garden now, at the end of the year.

Appendix I: Lists of Plant Ideas

Plants for:	Plants for:	Plants for:

Plants for:	Plants for:	Plants for:

Appendix II: Supplier Details

Name:		Date:
Postal Address:	URL:	
	User/Login:	
E-mail:	Password:	
☎	Notes	
☎		

Name:		Date:
Postal Address:	URL:	
	User/Login:	
E-mail:	Password:	
☎	Notes	
☎		

Name:		Date:
Postal Address:	URL:	
	User/Login:	
E-mail:	Password:	
☎	Notes	
☎		

Name:		Date:
Postal Address:	URL:	
	User/Login:	
E-mail:	Password:	
☎	Notes	
☎		

Name:		Date:
Postal Address:	URL:	
	User/Login:	
E-mail:	Password:	
☎	Notes	
☎		

Appendix III:
Ideas for Future Years

Thanks for choosing our Garden Planner. If you'd be willing to consider posting an Amazon review with a photo we'd be *most* grateful because many customers really struggle with loading the Look Inside facility.
We also publish affordable: Trip Planners, Reading Logs, Blank Recipe Books, Daily Planners, Academic Stationery & *much* more. To take a look, or get in touch, visit smartbookx.com.